making a difference

# Caring for your Pets

Jillian Powell

WAYLAND

# making a difference

# Caring for Others
# Caring for the Environment
# Caring for Your Pets
# Caring for Yourself

**Editor:** Sarah Doughty
**Designer:** Jean Wheeler

First published in 1997 by Wayland Publishers Ltd
61 Western Road, Hove, East Sussex BN3 1JD

Find Wayland on the internet at http:/www.wayland.co.uk

**British Library Cataloguing in Publication Data**
Powell, Jillian
Caring for your pets – (Making a Difference series)
1. Pets – Juvenile literature 2. Human-animal relationships –
Juvenile literature
I. Title
636'.0887

ISBN 0 7502 1944 0

Typeset by Jean Wheeler, in England
Printed and bound by G. Canale & C.S.p.A., Turin

**Picture acknowledgements**
Chris Fairclough 10 top, 14 bottom, 16 bottom, 21 top, 25; Cogis 9 (Francais); Oxford
Scientific 12 (G.I.Bernard), 15 (Michael Leach), 18 top (Keith Ringland), title page and 28
(Hans Reinhard/Okapia); Papilio Photographic 13, 14 top, 21 bottom, 23 top; Reflections 6, 7,
226 top, 27 (all by Jennie Woodcock); RSPCA 10 bottom, 24 bottom (both by Ken McKay), 16
top (Ian Jackson), 20 (Angela Hampton), 23 bottom (David Featherstone), 24 top (Ms Marina
Imperi), 26 bottom (Tim Sambrook); Tony Stone Worldwide 4 (Peter Correz), 5 (David Oliver),
8 (Kathi Lamm), 22 (Ian O'Leary); Wayland Picture Library 11, 18 (bottom), 19; Zefa 17
(P.Barton), 29. Cover commissioned photography by Angus Blackburn.

# Contents

Pets need to be loved and cared for, just like we do.

If you care for your pets, they will love you back.

Baby animals need special care.

If your pets are new and very young remember to be gentle with them.

A vet can check that your pet is healthy and give you advice on its care.

Some young pets need to have injections to stop them getting diseases.

They can be neutered to stop them having lots of babies.

Keep your pet's home clean by changing the straw or paper in a cage or hutch as soon as it gets dirty.

Put clean bedding in your pet's basket or bed.

A fish's tank is its home, so remember to keep the water clean.

Pets need fresh water to drink every day. Large animals like dogs and cats drink water from a bowl.

Animals that live in a cage or a hutch have a water bottle which they can drink from.

Find out what sort of food your pet should be eating. Know how often it needs to be fed.

Pets need
different types
of food to keep
them healthy
and take care
of their teeth,
eyes and coats.

Some pets need to have their hair or coats brushed. Keep a special comb or brush for your pet and wash it to keep it clean.

Some pets may need a
bath to keep them clean!

Pets sometimes have fleas living in their fur. Fleas make them itchy and they scratch themselves.

You can get rid of the fleas by using a special powder or spray on their coats and on their beds.

18

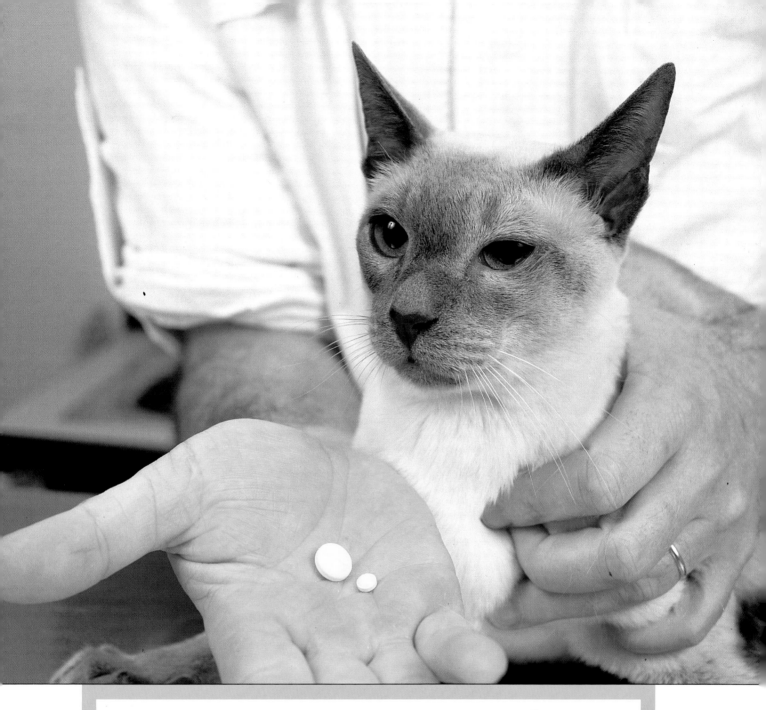

Some pets can get worms that live inside them. The vet can give you medicine which you put in their food to kill the worms.

Birds, cage animals and dogs
need to have their claws clipped
when they get too long.

Horses' hooves need to be clipped by a blacksmith every few weeks.

Rabbits may have to have their long front teeth clipped.

Pets need to play and exercise to keep them fit. Dogs need to be taken for a good walk every day.

All animals need space to run and play. Some animals can play in their cages; others need more space.

If your pet is ill or hurt,
you must take it to the vet.

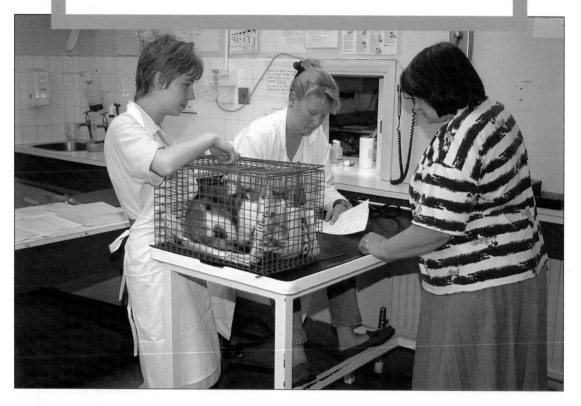

The vet will
be able to find
out what is
wrong and
may give your
pet medicine.

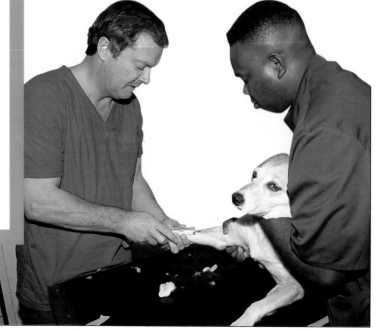

Your pet may need to stay in the vet's hospital for an operation. It will be well cared for.

Keep your pet safe at all times.
Make sure your pet cannot escape.

Dogs can die in
hot cars so never
leave your dog
in a car with the
windows shut on
a hot day.

Pets can be frightened or hurt
by fireworks so make sure they
stay indoors.

Find time to play with your pet.

Pets of all ages love playing and you can have lots of fun together.

# Extension activities

## MATHS

Design a class survey that will find out what kinds of pets children have or would like to have. Record your results in a graph form. Which pets are the most popular?

Different pets have different needs and habits. Discuss these and make a pictorial timetable to show what they do each day indicating feeding and exercise times.

Looking after pets requires providing them with food and bedding. Research the cost of these items, compare prices and weights and discuss value for money. Work out how much it costs to feed a pet per day, week, month and year. Which animal is the cheapest and which is the most expensive to keep?

## SCIENCE

Read labels on food packaging and information about caring for each pet to help you find out what food they need. Decide if the food is plant or animal based. Look for any physical features on the animal such as teeth and claws which may help you decide their eating preference in the wild. Make lists of the animals which you think are herbivores, carnivores or omnivores.

Classify pets into categories such as: mammals, birds and reptiles; pets with no legs, two or four legs; pets with or without teeth, or with beaks; pets with fur, feather or scale.

## R.E.

Using the slogan 'A PUPPY IS FOR LIFE NOT JUST FOR CHRISTMAS' discuss the long-term care and commitment required for pet ownership. Discuss whose responsibility caring for a pet should be; is it the children's, parent's or family's?

Compare the life expectancy of pets to each other and humans. Have any of the children experienced the death of a pet? Read and talk about books such as 'Scrumpy', 'I'll always love you', 'Fred', and 'Heaven' which may help children come to terms with their feelings.

Find out about St. Francis of Assisi.

Research the work of charitable organizations such as the RSPCA who care for the welfare of animals. Discuss the importance of getting pets through approved sources to minimise cruel practices such as illegal trapping and over-breeding.

## DESIGN AND TECHNOLOGY

Design a cage or pet carrier for your pet. Consider size, materials, bedding, feeding etc. Make labelled drawings from which to make a prototype.

Animals have often been used as design motifs to decorate walls and artefacts. Make a classroom display of any examples you can find. Can a particular animal make an object more or less desirable? With this in mind, design and make a gift which includes an animal shape or motif in its design.

## ENGLISH

In the imaginative play area establish a pet shop. Write booklets containing clear instructions on the care of each pet sold. Make labels and advertisements for the shop. During children's play encourage the use of informed discussion about, for example, the breed and temperament of each animal sold.

Make 'Who am I?' lift-the-flap cards, with a picture of an animal under the flap and a clue on the top such as 'I eat seeds, my plumage is blue or green, I can fly, what am I?'

## MUSIC

Listen to excerpts of music from compositions such as, 'Carnival of the Animals' and 'Peter and the Wolf'. Discuss how different instruments, sequences and tempo etc are used to portray the characteristics of each animal. Compose a short piece of music that describes your favourite pet.

## P.E./DANCE/DRAMA

Spend some time observing the habits and movements of one pet. You may want to take notes of particular mannerisms. How can you interpret these into a dance sequence?

Look at videos of animals. Focus on different methods of travelling across the floor, such as jumping, hopping, gliding and slithering. Practise control to improve your movements.

Improvise situations such as your neighbour who has left their dog in the car, on a hot day, with no ventilation. Consider what you should do, what you should say and how you should say it. What responses might the neighbour take?

## ART AND CRAFT

In the past wealthy people commissioned portraits of their pets as well as their families. Stubbs was famous for painting horses, Matisse painted a goldfish in its bowl. Find examples of animal paintings.

Using your own chosen media, depict your interpretation of a pet animal.

## GEOGRAPHY

Track down the original habitat and location of some of our pets such as parrots, budgerigars, cats, spiders and snakes. Can you pinpoint these places on a world map? Discuss the type of journey they would have to undergo if we allowed the importation of live animals. Discuss animal rights and welfare in relation to the livelihood of the animal traders.

## HISTORY

What can pet ownership tell us about the civilizations, or the socio-economic status of the people who owned them? Research pets in history. Where can evidence of their existence be found, which were the most popular and why? Are pets used or regarded in the same way today as they were in the past? Consider reasons for the changes in people's attitudes towards animals, such as function and cost.

## R.E.

- Discussing responsibility for care.
- Discussing life cycles and death.
- Finding out about St. Francis of Assisi.
- Discussing welfare charities.

## DESIGN AND TECHNOLOGY

- Designing a pet carrier.
- Designing a gift.

## ENGLISH

- Making labels and advertisements.
- Writing instructions.
- Discussing breeds.
- Making lift-the-flap cards.

## GEOGRAPHY

- Discussing countries of origin.

## HISTORY

- Researching pets in history.

# Caring for your Pets
Topic web

## MUSIC

- Listening to music.
- Composing music.

## SCIENCE

- Looking at labels for animal foods.
- Deciding on plant or meat eaters.
- Classifying pets.

## MATHS

- Designing a survey.
- Making a graph.
- Making a pictorial timetable.
- Comparing prices and weights.

## P.E./DANCE/DRAMA

- Animal movements.
- Creating dance sequences.
- Improvisations.

## ART AND CRAFT

- Looking at animal portraits.
- Portraying a pet.

# Glossary

**blacksmith**  Someone who looks after horses' hooves and fits their shoes.

**injection**  Medicine given to an animal using a needle.

**neutered**  When a pet has had an operation so it won't have babies.

# Books to read

*How To Look After Your Pet ...* series by Mark Evans (Dorling Kindersley 1990-2, p/b 1996)

*Me and My Pet Cat* by Christine Morley (Twocan, 1996)

*Me and My Pet Dog* by Christine Morley (Twocan, 1996)

# Index